Transportation & Communication Series

Trains

Phyllis J. Perry

Enslow Publishers, Inc.

40 Industrial Road   PO Box 38
Box 398   Aldershot
Berkeley Heights, NJ 07922   Hants GU12 6BP
USA   UK

http://www.enslow.com

*The publisher wishes to thank Laura S. Jeffrey for
her efforts in researching and editing this book.*

Library of Congress Cataloging-in-Publication Data

Perry, Phyllis Jean.
    Trains / Phyllis J. Perry.
        p. cm. — (Transportation & communication series)
Includes bibliographical references and index.
    ISBN 0-7660-1645-5
    1. Railroads—Juvenile literature. 2. Railroads—Trains—Juvenile
literature. [1. Railroads. 2. Railroads—Trains.] I. Title. II. Series.

    TF148 .P38 2001
    385—dc21   00-011560

Printed in the United States of America

10 9 8 7 6 5 4 3 2 1

To Our Readers:
We have done our best to make sure all Internet addresses in this book were active and appropriate when we went
to press. However, the author and the publisher have no control over and assume no liability for the material
available on those Internet sites or on other Web sites they may link to. Any comments or suggestions can be sent
by e-mail to comments@enslow.com or to the address on the back cover.

Every effort has been made to locate all copyright holders of material used in this book. If any
errors or omissions have occurred, corrections will be made in future editions of this book.

Illustration Credits: © Corel Corporation, pp. 10, 12, 14, 15, 16, 18, 19, 20, 22, 23, 24, 27, 30,
32, 33 (top), 34, 36, 39, 40, 41; Enslow Publishers, Inc., pp. 6, 28; Hemera Technologies, Inc.
1997–2000, pp. 1, 2, 5, 7, 11, 13, 17, 21, 25, 26, 29, 31, 33 (bottom), 35, 37, 38, 43, 47; Library
of Congress, p. 8; Stanford University Library, p. 4; Stanford University Museum of Art AAA, Gift of
David Hewes, p. 9.

Cover Illustration: © Corel Corporation

Contents

Chapter 1

Uniting a Nation

Trains carried people and freight before there were cars or planes. Railroads linked large cities, towns, and even coasts before today's roads and airports.

In 1850, California became part of the United States. But there was no easy way to go to the West. The United States Congress began thinking about how and where to build a transcontinental railroad. (Transcontinental means "across the land.") States talked about the best way for the railroad to go.

On July 1, 1862, President Abraham Lincoln signed the Pacific Railroad Act. This

Building the railroad was dangerous. Here a crew from the Central Pacific works on the track (left).

act said who would build the transcontinental railroad. It also told where the railroad would be built. Two companies were chosen to build the railroad: the Central Pacific Railroad and the Union Pacific Railroad.

Workers for the Central Pacific began building from the west. They started in Sacramento, California. Workers for the Union Pacific began building from the east. They started in Omaha, Nebraska. Work began in 1863.

More than twenty thousand men worked on the transcontinental railroad. They laid the track with their hands. More than ten thousand Chinese immigrants worked for the Central Pacific. Immigrants from Europe worked for the Union Pacific. (An immigrant is a person who goes to live in a country where he or she was not born.) Many soldiers who were in the Civil War also helped build the railroad.

Union Pacific Railroad started from the east. Central Pacific Railroad started building from the west.

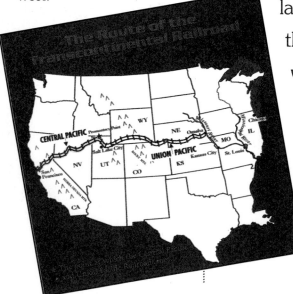

Building the railroad was dangerous work. The men faced very bad weather, attacks by American Indians, and accidents caused by explosions. They blasted through mountains. They worked under the hot desert sun and they worked very long hours.

The government promised money and land to the railroad companies. The amount was based on how much track was laid. This promise led to a contest. Each company wanted to lay more track than the other. In their rush to lay the most tracks, the railroad companies almost built past each other. The United States Congress wanted them to agree to a meeting point. The meeting point was going to be Promontory, Utah.

By early May 1869, the transcontinental railroad was almost finished. A train from the Central Pacific Railroad left California. It began traveling on the western track. A train from the Union Pacific left Nebraska. It began traveling on the eastern track. The trains were

Railroad workers used devices like these to make explosions. They could blast through mountains.

filled with important people from the railroad companies and others who wanted to ride the train.

On May 10, 1869 the transcontinental railroad was done. Here people gather around to watch the last spikes driven into the track.

On the morning of May 10, 1869, the trains met in Promontory, Utah. Hundreds of people got off the trains to watch as workers linked the two tracks. Then important men

from the railroad companies picked up a hammer to drive the last four spikes into the track. Two spikes were made of gold and the other two were made of silver.

Leland Stanford of the Central Pacific Railroad picked up a hammer to pound the final spike in place. He swung—and missed. Thomas C. Durant of the Union Pacific Railroad tried, but he missed, too. Finally, two other men drove the spikes into the track. The railroad was finished.

The crowd cheered loudly. Train whistles blew, and a band played. A signal, called a telegraph message, was sent. People all over the country cheered as they heard the news. The Union Pacific had built 1,086 miles of track. The Central Pacific had built 690 miles of track. The transcontinental railroad was done, uniting two sides of a nation.

This is one of the spikes used in the ceremony at Promontory, Utah.

Chapter 2

How Trains Work

Trains are made up of many railroad cars and are pushed or pulled by a locomotive. Locomotives are powerful engines. Trains move along metal rails, or tracks, that are held up by wooden ties.

The train wheels have special rims, called flanges. Flanges keep the train wheels on the tracks. The whole system of track is called a railroad. Railroads can cover hundreds or even thousands of miles.

Each section of railroad track is controlled separately. A signal operator checks to make sure the track is clear. Then the operator sets

Train wheels have special rims called flanges. Here an engineer (left) is making sure the train is in good working order.

the signals and switches. On the train, the engineer waits for a signal. The signal tells when it is safe to go. Signals along the track tell the engineer when to slow down. The signals also tell if another train is near. On busy railroads today, computers set the signals and switches.

Horses were once used to pull trains. But then trains used steam power. Coal or wood was burned in a section of the locomotive called a firebox. The fire heated water in the locomotive's boiler. The boiling water turned

The first trains used steam to make them go. Coal or wood was burned to heat water in the boiler. The steam and hot gases came out of the train through a chimney.

into steam. The steam pushed a piston up into a cylinder. When the steam cooled and turned back into water, the piston moved down.

The piston was connected to rods. The rods were connected to the train wheels. The piston moved back and forth. This motion caused the rods to move the train's wheels. Steam and hot gases from the fire came out of the locomotive through the smoke stack.

Coal was used to power early train engines.

Keeping steam engines running well was hard work. They needed fuel and water. Trains had to stop about every 100 miles to get more fuel and water to make the steam. Years later, diesel trains with a different type of engine replaced steam trains.

Diesel trains became popular because they did not need to stop a lot to get fuel. Diesel engines use heat made by a piston squeezing air inside a cylinder. When air is pushed into a small space, it becomes very hot. The heat makes the diesel oil explode. Energy is let go, and the piston is pushed down. This motion drives the engine.

Today, most trains use diesel and electric power together. They are called diesel-electric locomotives. The engine uses fuel from a large tank for power. The engine drives an electric generator. The generator sends a current through a transformer to power the motors. The motors turn the wheels.

Electric trains are another type of train. A frame called a pantograph is on the train's

Diesel-electric trains are used today. They use fuel and electricity to make them go.

roof. The pantograph collects electricity from overhead wires. The electricity is passed through a transformer to motors. These motors power the train.

Some electric trains do not have a pantograph. These trains have a metal shoe on the bottom of the front of the train. This shoe picks up electricity from a third rail next to the track.

Electric trains are sometimes used in large cities. People use these trains to get from one place to another. Sometimes, the trains run underground. In some places, these trains are called subways. Computers in a central control room make the trains work.

Electric trains are very fast. They can run for a long time at a high speed. Electric trains are also quieter than diesel-electric trains, and they do not make as much pollution. They cost more to build than some other trains.

Trains also use electricity to make them go. A pantograph on top of the train collects electricity.

Many people in big cities use subways.

Chapter 3

Trains Through the Years

Some of the first trains were built in the 1500s. They were simple carts on tracks that were pulled by horses. People did not ride on them. In 1804, steam trains were invented in England. They carried coal and other goods. In 1825, people were finally able to ride on trains when the first passenger steam train was invented. This train also was built in England.

The first steam train in the United States, called the Tom Thumb, was built in 1830. A race between Tom Thumb and a horse was held in New York. Even though the horse

This early steam engine (left) could probably only pull small carts.

These men are putting this locomotive together in the late 1800s.

won, people wanted to ride on the Tom Thumb. Soon, other steam trains were built. They became faster and less troublesome. Old Ironsides was another famous American steam train. It was built in 1832.

In 1861, the Civil War, or War Between the States, began. Trains were used to carry soldiers and supplies. When the war ended in 1865, more railroads were built. Four years later, the transcontinental railroad was finished. In 1886, the United States government and railroad companies made rules about what a train could look like. All train cars and tracks had to be the same size and shape. These rules were made so that any train could use any track.

By the late 1930s, diesel-electric trains started to replace steam trains. They were cheaper, cleaner, and faster. The design of trains also changed. Trains became long and sleek, or streamlined. The Zephyr was one of these trains. It was streamlined and made of stainless steel. The Zephyr was on display at the Chicago

In the 1930s, trains became long and sleek.

World's Fair in 1934. On May 26, 1934, the Zephyr made history. It went from Denver, Colorado, to Chicago, Illinois, without stopping. This was more than a thousand miles. The Zephyr went very fast, too. It went more than 112 miles per hour. The Zephyr set a record for going the farthest and the fastest, without stopping.

People liked riding trains. But cars changed

A train from the 1940s.

that. People wanted to drive cars instead. When World War II began, in 1941, people could only use a certain amount of some things. During the war years, gas was one of these things. Soldiers needed the gas for their trucks, planes, and tanks. People could not buy enough gas for their cars, so they started riding trains again.

World War II ended in 1945. People went back to using their cars. Some people used subway trains in cities. But for long trips, many people used cars or planes. Trucks or planes were used to move goods from one place to another. Railroad companies went out of business. During the years before the 1960s, 62 companies closed.

In 1970, a railroad company called Amtrak started. Amtrak stands for "America, Travel and Track." Most people who take train trips use Amtrak. But in 1996, the Union Pacific

Cars started to become more popular than trains until there was a shortage of gasoline during the war years.

21

A train from the 1950s.

An electric train from the 1970s (right).

ran a special passenger train across the United States. The train carried people to the Olympic Games in Atlanta, Georgia. It also carried the Olympic torch.

In the United States today, cars, trucks, and planes are used the most. But many people still enjoy riding trains. In 1999, more than 21 million people took trips on Amtrak trains. Every day, about 265 trains go to 500 stations. They travel more than 22,000 miles.

Chapter 4

Many Ideas, Many People

Ideas and people made train travel happen. Two British men, Thomas Newcomen and James Watt, designed steam engines. These engines led to steam locomotives. Richard Trevithick of England built the first steam locomotive. Rudolph Diesel, a German, invented the diesel engine. Diesel locomotives replaced steam locomotives.

Another British train maker was George Stephenson. George and his son, Robert, made many steam trains. They were used all over the world. One of these trains was the Rocket. It was the first steam train to go within

This train makes it way through the snow (left).

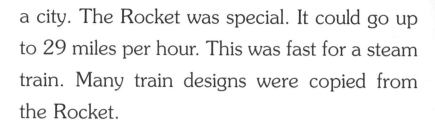

Trains became safer and more comfortable for travelers.

a city. The Rocket was special. It could go up to 29 miles per hour. This was fast for a steam train. Many train designs were copied from the Rocket.

The Tom Thumb was the first steam train in the United States. Peter Cooper built it. Other people made train travel safer and more comfortable. George Pullman invented a fancy train car. It became known as the Pullman car. It was the world's first sleeper car. George Westinghouse invented an automatic brake for trains. The brake worked by air pressure.

Inventors and engineers built the trains. Businessmen ran the large railroad companies. One famous railroad businessman was Cornelius Vanderbilt. He started as a shipping leader. When the Civil War began, he became interested in railroads. He ran the New York Central Railroad. His son, William Henry Vanderbilt, was also with the New York Central Railroad. The Vanderbilts were a very wealthy and well-known family.

Another important person was Theodore Judah. He built many railroads in the northeast. In 1854, he went to California. Judah found a way to lay tracks across the mountains in California. Now the transcontinental railroad could be built. Thomas C. Durant ran the Union Pacific Railroad.

As new trains came about they became famous. A famous American train was the Twentieth Century Limited. It ran from

A train from the 1860s.

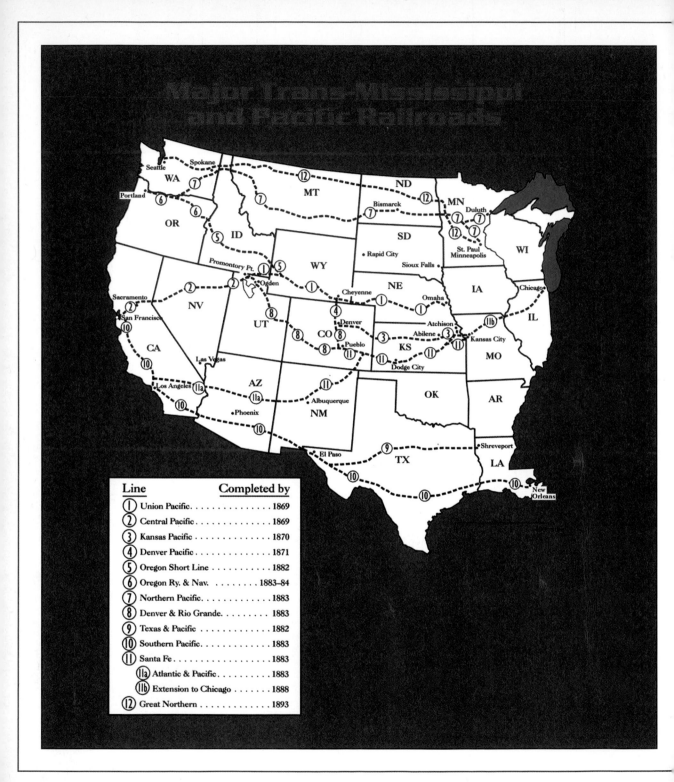

Major Trans-Mississippi
and Pacific Railroads

Line	Completed by
① Union Pacific...............	1869
② Central Pacific..............	1869
③ Kansas Pacific..............	1870
④ Denver Pacific.............	1871
⑤ Oregon Short Line..........	1882
⑥ Oregon Ry. & Nav.	1883–84
⑦ Northern Pacific...........	1883
⑧ Denver & Rio Grande........	1883
⑨ Texas & Pacific	1882
⑩ Southern Pacific............	1883
⑪ Santa Fe..................	1883
⑪ₐ Atlantic & Pacific........	1883
⑪ᵦ Extension to Chicago	1888
⑫ Great Northern.............	1893

New York City's Grand Central Station to Chicago, Illinois. Passengers boarding the train walked on a red carpet that was laid on the platform. The train had a barber shop and an observation car.

In Europe, the Orient-Express made its first run in 1883. It traveled from France to many other countries, including Turkey, Greece, and Egypt. The Orient-Express was very fancy. People who rode on the train had soft seats and the best food to eat.

The Orient-Express stopped service in 1977, but private companies have found and fixed some of the original train cars. The train is working again in Europe and the United States. The Orient-Express gives people the chance to enjoy fancy train travel once again.

The Orient-Express would go to such interesting places as Egypt.

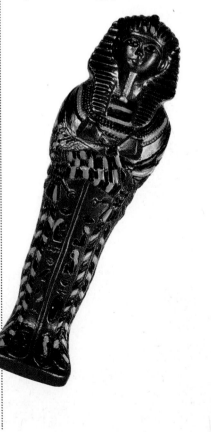

Chapter 5

Working on the Railroad

Do you want to take a train trip? Many people will work hard to make sure you have a safe and happy ride. The trains leave from a train station. At the train station, the station master is in charge. The station master makes sure everything is running well. Ticket agents, or sellers, sell tickets for train rides. They also tell people when trains will leave the station, and when others will arrive. If delays happen, ticket agents let passengers know that, too.

Trains cannot wait for late passengers. They must stay on time. Porters carry suitcases and help passengers board, or get

In the 1900s, many people worked on trains (left). A cook is standing in the doorway of the train. The conductor and the porter are standing on the ground.

on, the train. The conductor is the one who calls, "All aboard!" This is to warn people to get on the train because it will leave soon. The conductor stays on the train during the trip. He helps passengers find seats. The conductor also collects tickets. He tells riders when and where the train is stopping.

Other workers on the train make beds in sleeper cars. They cook and serve food in the

People riding the trains enjoyed sitting back and watching the world go by.

dining cars. When the train makes its final stop, they clean the train to get it ready for its next trip.

Before the train trip starts, some work has already been done. Train cars and equipment have been designed and built. Crews have laid the track and kept it in good working order. In snowy or icy weather, they clear the tracks. The train must go through.

Many people helped build railroads.

Other railroad workers have decided the train schedule. This means how often it will run. On train routes that are popular, trains run more often. This stops overcrowding. The cost of the ticket, or fare, also has to be decided. Other people advertise to get customers to ride their trains.

On passenger trains and freight trains, the engineer is the driver. Using levers, switches, and buttons, the engineer controls the train.

Computers help the engineer with his job. Computers also help to read signals along the tracks.

Some electric trains run by computer. These kinds of trains run in city subways. The computer is in a central control room. Everything on the train is automatic. The

City subway trains run automatically.

doors open and close by computer. The train starts and stops by computer. An engineer stays on the train to make sure nothing goes wrong. Sometimes, the engineer calls out the stops to the passengers.

When goods are moved, workers help fill and empty the train cars. When the train stops, workers sometimes add or take away cars. Switchmen and yardmen work in the railroad yards. Railroad yards are where trains stop to be loaded or unloaded. The workers move the cars around and hook them together.

Many people important to train travel can be seen doing their jobs. Others work but you will not see these people when you take a train ride. They are working just as hard to make train travel safe.

Trains are used to ship goods and packages.

Chapter 6

Back to the Future

Many people have stopped riding trains. They take trips by airplane or car. Many businesses have stopped using trains to move goods. They, too, use airplanes. They also use trucks. But people may want to use trains again. Highways are full of cars and trucks. Many people do not like driving on them. They want to read or rest while taking a trip. They do not want to worry about traffic or road repairs.

Promontory, Utah (left), is now a National Historic site because in 1869, two railroads became one—the transcontinental railroad.

Fast electric trains do not pollute the air with gasoline fumes.

Trucks and cars make pollution. Drivers pay high prices for gas. Sometimes there is not enough. Trucks and cars make more pollution than trains do. And planes use more fuel than trains. All of these things may make people use trains once more.

Many people think high-speed electric trains are needed. They go faster than cars. They do not pollute the air. And they are more comfortable and relaxing for passengers. In 1999, Amtrak began testing these trains in parts of the United States. Acela Express, Amtrak's first high-speed train, made its first run in November 2000. The train goes from Washington, D.C., to Boston, Massachusetts, and can go up to 150 miles per hour.

In other countries, high-speed trains have been used for decades. Sometimes these trains use tracks already in place. Other times, special tracks are built.

Japan has used high-speed trains for almost forty years. These are called bullet trains. They are made of aluminum and are lightweight and speedy. Germany also has high-speed trains. They go as fast as 174 miles per hour. High-speed trains in Italy go as fast as 190 miles per hour. The tracks in Italy have few curves. Straight tracks let the train keep up its high speeds.

The newest high-speed trains do not have wheels. This makes them go even faster. These trains are called magnetic levitation, or maglev, trains. Maglev trains use magnetic

Japan has used bullet trains like these for almost forty years.

This is a *train a grande vitesse*, or TGV. It is a high-speed train in Paris, France.

forces to move. They are very good for going far and can go as fast as 300 miles per hour. Germany and Japan already use maglev trains. And in 1996, a maglev train opened in Walt Disney World. Perhaps one day soon, maglev trains will be used everywhere.

Trains are exciting. People all over the country join clubs to talk about trains. They collect miniature, or small, trains. They set up old train sets. They put on shows all over the country. Other people enjoy coming to these shows. They like to imagine what old train travel was like. Sometimes it makes them want to take a trip on today's trains.

The days of steam trains may never return. That would not be useful. But it is very likely that one day, using high-speed, and maglev trains will be just like using cars and planes.

Many people collect model trains.

 41

Timeline

1500s—Horses pull trains, which are carts on tracks.

1804—The steam train is invented in England.

1833—Orient-Express makes its first trip.

1861—Civil War begins. Trains are used to help soldiers.

1862—President Abraham Lincoln signs Pacific Railroad Act.

1863—Work begins on the transcontinental railroad.

1865—Civil War ends; More railroads are built.

May 10, 1869—Transcontinental railroad is done.

Timeline

Late 1930s—Diesel-electric trains begin to replace steam trains.

1934—New streamlined Zephyr is shown at Chicago's World Fair.

1970—America, Travel and Track (Amtrak) starts.

1996—Union Pacific Railroad runs a special train carrying the Olympic torch to the 1996 Olympic Games in Atlanta, Georgia; Maglev train opens in Walt Disney World.

1999—Amtrak begins testing high-speed trains in the United States.

2000—Acela Express, Amtrak's high-speed train makes its first run.

Words to Know

caboose—A railroad car that is at the end of a train.

Civil War—In the United States, the Civil War (1861–1865) was fought between Northern and Southern states.

coach—A type of railroad car that carries people. Also called a carriage.

cylinder—A tube that serves as the piston chamber of an engine.

dispatcher—A person who sends official, speedy messages directing the route and working of a train.

flange—A rim on a train wheel that guides and helps keep the train in place on the track.

freight—Cargo, or goods, shipped from one place to another.

generator—A machine that produces electricity, steam, or other energy.

gondola car—A railroad car with sides and ends without a top. It is used to carry freight in large amounts. Can also be called a wagon.

Words to Know

immigrant—A person who comes to live in a country where he or she was not born.

locomotive—An engine that moves on its own power. It is used to pull or push railroad cars.

monorail—A train that runs on or is suspended from a single rail that is its track.

piston—A cylinder that fits closely inside a tube or hollow cylinder where it moves back and forth. The movement of the piston in a train engine moves the train's wheels.

pollution—Harmful materials such as chemicals, gases, and wastes that dirty the air, water, or soil.

track—A set of rails on which the trains move.

transcontinental—Spanning, or crossing, the continent.

World War II—A war between 1939 and 1945 mainly fought in Europe, North Africa, and Asia. The United States entered World War II in 1941, and it united with Great Britain, France, the Soviet Union, China, and their allies to fight against Nazi Germany, Japan, and Italy.

45

Learn More About
Trains

Books

Brady, Peter. *Freight Trains*. Mankato, Minn.: Bridgestone Books, 1996.

Otfinoski, Steven. *Riding the Rails: Trains Then and Now*. New York, N.Y.: Benchmark Books, 1997.

Oxlade, Chris. *Train*. Parsippany, N.J.: Silver, Burdett & Ginn, Inc., 1999.

Richards, Jon. *Trains*. Brookfield, Conn.: Copper Beech Books, 1998.

Stille, Darlene R. *Trains*. Danbury, Conn.: Children's Press, 1997.

Learn More About
Trains

Internet Addresses

Central Pacific Railroad Photographic History Museum
<http://cprr.org>

See pictures of the building of the first transcontinental railroad.

How Steam Engines Work
<http://www.howstuffworks.com/steam.htm>

Find out how steam engines work. Great diagrams.

National Railroad Historical Society
<http://www.nrhs.com>

Check out Historic Rail Photos for great photos of trains.

Union Pacific Railroad: It's Just Railroad Talk
<http://www.uprr.com/uprr/ffh/rrtalk>

Check out this site from the Union Pacific Railroad and learn Railroad talk.

Index